MAN MADE MYTHS

THOUGHT TRIGGERS

CHIRAAG ASHOK BHATT

This book is dedicated to my late dad Ashok C Bhatt, his blessings has always helped me grow further in my life.

Also will like to dedicate to my mom Jigisha Ashok Bhatt, my prime source of daily motivation.

Will like to dedicate to my younger brother Sanjay Ashok Bhatt, he was the one who triggered the title which later triggered me to build this book further along with Sachin.

Contents

1. Introduction 1

2. Relegions & Avatars 2

3. The Purpose Of The Holy Places? 4

4. What Is High Blood Pressure 7

5. Do We Have Powers To Self-heal? 9

6. Are Ghost Real 11

7. What Is Aura 13

8. Sub-conscious Mind Power 15

9. What Are Chakras Can We Actually Activate It? 17

10. Who Is Yogi? 19

11. Are We Living The Right Life? 20

12. What Is Karma? 23

13. Why Is It Mother / Father / Guru And God? 25

14. Relationship & Money 27

15. About The Author – Chiraag Ashok Bhatt 29

16. About The Co-author – Sachin Sajan 30

CHAPTER ONE

INTRODUCTION

In this book, we bring to you some important thought triggers that will help in revisiting what we have learned or thought from our childhood. If those were the right knowledge or do we further need to dig deeper to get a better understanding. Though what is mentioned in this book is purely our perception and not to disturb anyone's sentiment or learning. It is to inculcate a thought that why don't we think in this direction as well, it might either prove the point right or will help us build further information. In this era of free knowledge and wisdom available on the internet, we need to self-educate and not believe things blindly. We hope you find this book interesting and will keep you engaged and trigger the inner you who is very much talented than you actually understand. Give the inner you these thoughts and see the different you in all the aspects. Learning is forever, there are good learnings as well as bad learnings, its from where we learn and how much we take it in and how much we ignore. With the above introduction, let's go further, we hope the information from this book helps you with different perception and let's build a better place around us with more of sharing and building knowledge.

CHAPTER TWO

RELEGIONS & AVATARS

Everything has its origin, and so do religion and the gods associated with each known religion. But, have you ever wondered how faith came into existence and how each of us is born within particular beliefs? It's not like a magical hat will be put on our heads to decide which group we belong to. That would have been fun. It seems magical hats can only be witnessed in the harry potter universe and not in real life. The reason why one cannot choose their religion can be simply put as they are born into one. One is not choosing their parents just the same way the parents are not choosing the children, but they're brought into this world with a bond of relation and a religion.

Each of us, at a point, will question many things in life that will make us more human, and while we do that, some of us will question why do religions exist?

All we can say is that we have all come to this earth with a purpose which we do not know, hence the basics of religion are to support in building us up, parents / guardians support in building us up furthermore, a boss helps you to build up furthermore and kids reflect what you have learned and passed on to them. Do you understand how profound this point is and now think are you doing justice to the birth you are blessed with.

Religions are for bringing discipline in life, name any religion, and you will find this concept of discipline. If followed well, there are many more that it teaches.

Do you ever think about Avatars or Incarnations, who were also born as humans and later on learned the ways of a normal human being, yet they are completely different and can do things that normal human beings cannot imagine doing. The reason for this is simply that they have known the purpose of their existence and the power their bodies possess since birth.

If we just study the Avatars or Incarnations' life stories, it gives us a path to solve any issues we are stuck in our life. Learning about all avatars and incarnations is very critical to leading a meaningful life, hence this brings us to an important point that every religion has knowledge that needs to be learned by us and not restricting or fighting for it. Every piece of knowledge will be helpful if not immediate but by the end of your life for sure.

All of us have powers, it's all blocked because we have chosen them to be blocked. Hence there is a saying that if you religiously follow or believe in something it's bound to succeed.

I hope we are all on the same page as we dig deeper and put aside the fights in the name of religion, and stop blaming our parents saying they did not take care of us, stop blaming our bosses, stop blaming our kids for growing up bad, all these are because of the choices we make. You can choose to change today for a better tomorrow.

CHAPTER THREE

The Purpose of the Holy Places?

Have you ever wondered about the reasons for holy places to exist and why are we being asked to go there?

We, humans, get sick and we are taken to the hospital where we are brought to the attention of a doctor and then that person helps us recover. Visiting a holy place is like going to a doctor. All-holy places have a very senior person who has dedicated his life to learning it fully. They will have knowledge of all religions, for health ailments, as doctors can give you medicines, for life ailments holy places act like your doctors, it's important that we have a positive vibration environment to pep up our inner soul. All the Holy places with all the right practice done daily are the most positive space for our inner cleansing.

Any problem we're stuck up in life, we usually take it to the senior person at the holy place, they will guide us to what can be the best solution with stories and examples of avatars or incarnations who handled similar problems in their life when they lived, this might not give you an immediate solution but a perspective to think and solve your issues in a much better mode.

Another point why they are made is it can be a place where all with similar mindsets can be under one roof. It's similar to a multi-speciality hospital.

Hence it's very important we respect all the holy places and we do not disturb their peace, if disturbed, it can create a ripple effect which can lead to many other issues in connection to it.

You might also have thoughts that these holy places have become commercial and only mint money. This thought is justified as the question may arise, why would God need money?

Yes! God doesn't need money but the place one finds his or her peace has a few expenses to take care of and to tackle those, these places need money.

There are places where you can contribute with not just money but your services but if you are someone who doesn't find that much time then these places accept contributions from your end of any kind. No one forces anyone to pay a fee to be greeted by these places. It's a personnel choice. We pay from the bottom of our hearts and help the holy place grow. Imagine if you don't expect anything and just solution of life and learn all the good things, and don't need a VIP line for a faster solution, if your god loving and not god-fearing you will not need to give big, as life is common for all, it is how large or small you make it.

When it comes to the holy place one is always treated equally. As one demands special treatments these places have come up with solutions to make your visit special. The holy place is again working for you and also making the place bigger.

Next time when you go to a holy place, stop spending money and start learning, holy places actually don't need your money. You can start the change, instead, feed the hungry, God is all around, God does not need your money, God only needs you to be good to people around and God will ensure all the good deeds comes back to you.

CHAPTER FOUR

What is High Blood Pressure

We have heard more about this BP, have you ever thought about it in a general sense, yes let me break the ice further this can trigger a lot more things in your thought process.

Blood flows to all parts of the body, it is designed so well that it takes all the important essence of our food post-process to all parts of the body and gives specific needs to specific parts of the body.

The main engine behind is our Heart, which keeps pumping day in and day out helping all parts of our body get what it needs, oh yes, our body is so well connected (For Eg. If the joint of the leg has pain, there is a message sent to the heart, please send me VIT D urgently, the heart will be pumping normal for the 1st request if the request is repeated, the heart keeps pumping faster leading to High BP, yes its because there is no VIT D it does not know what to do, it will keep beating faster till the joint stops the request)

Made it a straightforward example for making you understand in an easy method, with which you will understand the context coming up further easily.

Our body needs a consistent perfect intake of food with all tastes in your regular diet, which will help all the essence in the blood to be always available. There are 6 tastes of food if taken every day, our body will not only function well but also will be so resistant that it can fight any big diseases.

Your tongue also sometimes alarms or request you to feed a taste in, you must have got a feeling of eating something spicy, sweet, sour, etc. So we can also call our Tongue our prelim doctor. Isn't our body very interesting if we keep digging, we will keep learning more.

Blood Pressure is a creation of ours, if we don't follow the perfect diet according to our body, then there will be a time when the speed dial will have a doctor's number. If you want to handle it yourself it's still possible, you can if you want to, the ball is always in your court.

CHAPTER FIVE

Do we have powers to self-heal?

What is self-healing? The power of your brain is not used by us at all, keep reading it will surprise you for sure, from chapter 1 what is being explained in this chapter is all interconnected, realize your power and you will see the difference.

Let me tell you a tale to make you understand better.

There was once a cancer patient who, even after getting all the best treatment out there wasn't able to recover, he kept suffering that was because we have it all in our mind that cancer isn't curable. We have been made to believe that cancer is something which will come to our doors, knock on them and take us with it. He had the same thing in his mind, cancer is not curable and there is no medicine for it.

Once he was going through the news that a medicine has been discovered and it can heal cancer. The patient calls the doctor and asks him about this medicine, the doctor says yes they are testing it and its working, in all happiness patient asks for that medicine and the doctor agrees to him the medicine by tomorrow, doctor checks with the manufacturer and comes to know that it has not got the approval and is in the testing stage. Testing stage medicine is never prescribed. Then the doctor had an idea and was thought to make use of the confidence of the patient that he had in this medicine. The very next day the doctor comes to the patient and says I am going to inject that medicine and you're going to be free from cancer. The patient was very happy and got the medicine injected, then the doctor asked him to take good rest and told let's see the developments. The doctor knew it was just a normal medicine that was injected. A few days passed by and to his surprise, there were developments and in a few weeks cancer disappeared from the body and the patient was discharged, the doctor was also surprised and he was happy that the patient inner confidence has helped him heal and did not reveal him the trick used on him.

After a few months, the same patient had seen the news that the cancer medicine didn't qualify to be used on the patients. This news started building doubts in him, resulting in, cancer was formed in his body and was admitted to the hospital, doctors were surprised and later on, he passed away.

This story is a trigger for all of us, to believe that our body can heal with the power of our mind, we need to boost the mind with more confidence and believe anything is possible.

CHAPTER SIX

Are Ghost real

In existence, there are both positive and negative forces. This is like the theory for every action there is always an opposite reaction.

If we just give it a little perspective and assume positive force is Good and Negative is Evil.

When you do good things good happen to you and when you only start thinking bad for others and even done anything bad actually is enough to disturb and the negativity starts haunting you.

You must be pondering what logic is this, are we talking about ghosts or deeds, there is actually no difference.

The more positive you are the negative can't disturb you, the more negative you are, and you start attracting more and more negative energies towards you.

Yes, negative energy is like a ghost. It's only a form of energy and does not have flesh and blood, it's capable of creating fear and disturbing your mind. As things go on, you start becoming like the energy.

The person with good positive energy can only help such an affected person, you call them Ghostbusters / Physiatrist. The main thing common in them is they enforce as much as they know to cure the affected individual, the prime strength of theirs is the positivity they carry. It's the strength that positivity and determination to win over the negative.

Hence, they ask for the details of the person affected, how it started, how was his upbringing, did he have any episodes of depression in his past etc. Before even handling the person, they hypnotise and get the information from within.

Thought is triggered, now this will kindle the need to know more, keep digging, finding and sharing knowledge.

CHAPTER SEVEN

What is Aura

In simple terms, around our body there is an invisible field that always exists, this is very important, let me iterate with an example which all off us can definitely relate to as it would have definitely occurred in each of our lives.

When someone you like the most or dislike the most is around or near you, without you seeing them you start to get the feeling of them around you, and after sometime you find the person in front of you. Have you ever wondered how this happens?

Yes, you guessed it right, you are not human! Just kidding, it's their Aura, that helps you sense it when the Aura of the other person is around your aura also has a memory and helps you feel it. See how powerful this is.

Therefore it's very important we keep our Aura healthy, how can it be done?

Aura needs to be cleansed regularly there are a few ways,

- **Water Cleansing**

You would feel refreshed when you go under a waterfall or a good shower, unknowingly you're cleansing your Aura.

- **Wind Cleansing**

When there is a fresh and good breeze you feel refreshed, this also cleanses your Aura.

- **Meditation**

When you meditate every morning, your aura starts to expand, start doing this every day.

What way Aura Helps you is when you meet anyone for the first time, you also create something called Aura impact, also known as "Vibe" these days.

The better your aura the better your first interaction even before starting your communication as the opposite person Aura gets attracted to good Aura, leading to healthy and fruitful discussions, and making it positive towards you.

Start working on your Aura, do as much good to people around you, and your Aura will keep becoming powerful. As mentioned above keep cleansing your Aura regularly.

Thought is triggered now it's your time to dig deep and use the benefits.

CHAPTER EIGHT

Sub-conscious mind power

Imagine for a moment how powerful your subconscious mind is. When you think of a challenge and is in desperate search of a solution, you will get a sudden idea, it's the power of your subconscious mind! This part of the mind is active 24x7 even when you are at sleep.

Here's a challenge for you, try it out. If there's a problem you have and aren't able to find a solution for it, just think about it before you sleep. The subconscious mind starts helping you find the solution as you are asleep, and the solution might come in your dream or the next day when you're thinking about it.

You must be wondering reading the book for so long, do our bodies have so many capabilities? Yes, it does, but the only reason we were not aware of these is just that we never gave a thought to all these subjects.

The more we dig the more we find the unknown. It's very important to keep digging deeper to discover new things every day.

How to build a strong subconscious mind will be your next question right? It's very important we train this part of the mind for being highly productive, this part of the mind also gives us intuitions.

To make it powerful here are the simple rules.

Meditation – When you close your eyes you must come to a state where no thoughts disturb you and you are able to tell your mind what to do.

It is very difficult but it isn't impossible. Initially, the moment you close your eyes, there will be so many thoughts hovering around, the best way to train it.

This practice of meditation will start making you stable, this will also start to reflect in your daily life. While handling challenges you must take one step at a time, and during solving challenges, when your subconscious mind starts giving you options then you will be able to realize the power your subconscious mind holds.

Thought is triggered, now time to dig deeper and gain the benefits.

CHAPTER NINE

What are chakras can we actually Activate it?

There are 7 chakras in our body, and there are many tips out there to activate it, for this you will need an advisor or guru. If you follow basis the guidance of the tips, sometimes if your body is pre-programmed and has its memory it can work to your benefit, but how do we find this out? This question must arise. The best suggestion is having an advisor or guru who is already practising it.

What will happen if we activate all the chakras? It can be dangerous. If you're leading a life with commitments and a family and unlocking the chakra will take you to a different state of mind with no interest in the world, it's not that you will become insane, it's just that you will start seeing things and the world around you very differently, you will be becoming a source of knowledge and wisdom without barriers.

Nothing will be impossible for a person who activates the 7 chakras, yes, it's true, they can control their body aging, any defect in the body can correct themselves, and they can help heal others as well. You must be wondering do they become superhuman, we are already super and blessed being born human, what is to notice is that they have found their path of life.

But there is a statutory warning as mentioned earlier, people who activate their 7 chakras are generally alone and do whatever they feel like, it's difficult for them to adjust to the normal way of life as they are way above all of them by thoughts and actions.

Hence thought is triggered, now you can decide to dig deeper and choose your path and findings.

CHAPTER TEN

Who is Yogi?

Anyone can become a yogi, but the rules are very different and tough, whatever you have read so far, if you hear about these from a yogi, you will have more and more insights flowing through you. They can be your guru to help you build further.

Their mind is connected to the cosmos. Have you ever thought, the technology which we have today never existed but still then our yogis were able to tell the number of planets and their positions! It is believed that they could leave their body and travel anywhere to get the information and come back to their body. You would have heard some theories of Astral Projections etc. They are the ones that can make it a possibility.

It might be very interesting to become a yogi, but it's not at all that easy, hence lets practice some of the basics of a yogi lifestyle, let's practice yoga regularly, which can help us keep our body fit, this is much better than going to the gym, believe me, it gives you resistance, it gives you stamina, it helps good blood flow all through your body, in a nutshell, you will be away from all major diseases, well that's a need of hour.

Now the thought is triggered, now you can decide to dig deeper and choose your path and findings.

CHAPTER ELEVEN

Are we living the right life?

This is a very important thing today, living the right life! While this has many definitions from different sources, I believe in making it very simple as always.

"If we take care of people around us, the good deeds will take care of us"

Isn't it very interesting and simple?

It starts from our home. Always.

Parents – Please take the best care of them, their blessings will keep you rocking all through your life. It can be very simple things, spending time with them, telling them to rest and giving them assurance you are there for them as they have made you self-reliant sacrificing their life, send them on holiday and let them also enjoy.

Siblings - You being younger or older than your siblings, it does not matter, what matters the most is staying together during the ups and downs. They are your first friend in life, thus we can't let go of a friend, can we? The benefit of staying together is always on the winning side, as your expenses are shared, your burden is shared, and even if any of your siblings are not on good terms now he/she will come to understand the godsends in the latter part of life. What you can do is, stand behind them as a pillar irrespective of whatever treatment you get, build a bigger heart and forgive them as they are your blood.

Relatives – All of us have relations, some good, some bad, but if you dig deeper, they are bad because they don't take the extra effort to think from your shoes and think things only from their perception and keep bullying you.

What we can do is ignore and keep ourselves unaffected by them. It's the mindset that helps us become strong characters. With good relatives be grateful. For the bad ones, It's just a matter of time, when karma makes them realize their mistake and they might change in due course of time. The other thing we can do is keep the door open for good and neglect it for the bad and not curse as there will be no difference between you and them.

WIFE / HUSBAND – For the wife, she must step in the role of mother of the boy, similarly for the Husband he must take the role of the father of the girl. When this is followed there is actually no scope for fight at home. The Girl will behave responsibly taking care of the husband's parents at home and the responsibility of the house. When a girl does this the boy feels he is blessed and focuses more to bring up the family and does all best to keep her happy like her father used to. It's like karma, when we do all this when kids are born they actually see all this and they treat you the same way when you are in your older days of life, as I said in the earlier chapter, what you learn reflects in your kids, hence please think 100 times before you act, if you respect all the elders and give importance to their happiness, the kids will be respecting you, kids of this generation are way advanced, they are very intelligent and catch up things very quickly. Hence thought is triggered please work on this for a healthy retired life. It's not money you need in your old days its people you need like suggested you spend more time with parents same will be your seeking with your kids.

Office / Co-workers / Friends – Very beautiful relation these are, as this is where the other half of your life is spent while the other half is family, what can you do is much more, in this part of your life. Please earn as many people as you can, yes you read it right it's not money it's people that you need to earn. When you have more people around money is a by-product, believe me, it's real.

It's not about the money you earn in your life, it's the impact that creates with your existence that needs to be earned in your life. When you leave this life, how many people remember you matter the most, your money hardly matters.

What you can do is, help as many as you can of course within your means and not beyond, sometimes standing by stating moral support, "I'm there for you", and "you can do it" makes a great difference. Also, don't buy a relationship with money, if you feel you have many around you that's because of your money, the moment it's away all is gone like a dream. Choose your people around you very well. Create an environment of happiness and knowledge sharing, and avoid bitching and backstabbing. Thoughts are triggered its time for you to dig deeper to find your path further.

CHAPTER TWELVE

What is Karma?

All of us have heard the statement, "what goes around comes around", it's very true, also making us believe that there is no heaven and hell.

The life that you living has both exists parallelly, yes you read it right, when you do good deeds and don't hurt anyone in your life, you might get into the hard phase of life which will teach you things. You get out of it with the support of people around you, you might get help from places where you never expected that's a good thing of karma. Now the other side, if you even think bad for anybody it starts coming to you, and if you have done bad to anyone, then be ready it might come back to you strong, or it might affect anyone really close to you.

Do we need all these, Let's lead a life setting an example and not becoming an example to people of not living such a life.

Karma = Actions

What actions you're doing or planning to do, it's important from today we think multiple times, are we doing it for goodwill? Will, it affects anyone's life, feelings, etc. When you do so, there is no judge required to actually help you decide as your mind is very powerful to gauge things easily.

There is no point in going to holy places and seeking forgiveness, the best way to subside the karma is to seek forgiveness from the person who is affected by your actions. God is everywhere, it's just that you are closing your eyes and seeking him. When you live life the way it must be lived, you will be the source of motivation for people around you.

Thought is triggered, now it's time for you to dig deeper and find your path of life.

CHAPTER THIRTEEN

Why is it Mother / Father / Guru and God?

Have you ever thought about this fact, that is thought to us from our childhood? These are followed from years, if you dig deeper, I found the following which are interesting.

Mother – She is first because you have existed on this earth because of her, now imagine how thankful you must be to her to bring you to this wonderful world.

Father – He is the next important person, who shelters you till you stand on your feet; he acts like your backbone. Every father's dream is very simple, his family must be happy always and kids must become self-dependent. For this he goes to any extent of sacrifice. Now imagine how grateful and thankful you must be to him to bring you to this wonderful world and stay right behind you to be a complete man or woman.

To understand the value of parents please ask any orphan how he/she feels by not having them around. Please refrain from finding reasons that they are good or bad, it's important to be grateful just for the fact that you are born because of them. Another aspect actually really doesn't matter as it can be managed in the due course of time.

Guru - This is a very important person. They teach you the lessons of life and guide you on the things in the outside world. They are like testimonies, it helps us to understand and prepare ourself before dealing the real world.

God – Why God comes last is, he is a creator, the best teachers can be the ones who have lived it through as their experience can't be matched by GOD.

If you see stories of incarnation, even God goes through all these stages.

Thought is triggered, now it's time for you to dig deeper and find your path.

CHAPTER FOURTEEN

Relationship & Money

What is that you choose from the above, as these are the 2 classes of people that exist in this planet.

To those who have chosen Relationship, they understand the value of life and they will never have problem of money in their life, this does not mean they will be super rich, they will have enough to lead their life as they are very content in nature and does not need all luxury amenities in life.

This group of people who have chosen a relationship will have peace of mind, a great and big family together, healthy life, no regret, many people around them, and never feel left alone.

Now those who have chosen Money, do not understand valuc of life, because they will be busy finding ways to make money, and they will not have time to spend even with their families. They would have not taken this route by choice but by default, as the situation might have demanded the same. What happens to them is, they will get bored of life soon, as they do not have anything else other than money as a focus in life, they choose people around as well who can help them build wealth, people like this are ruthless and the circle is also ruthless, advice to these group of people will identify what is actually required, in the sense come to a figure that is actually required, it will surprise you that you don't need to waste your all your life and move to the relationship group.

When you're in-Relationship group money actually starts becoming the by-product. With a healthy life with good people around you everything falls in place.

Thought is triggered, now it's time for you to dig deeper and find your path.

CHAPTER FIFTEEN

ABOUT THE AUTHOR – Chiraag Ashok Bhatt

CHIRAAG ASHOK BHATT, Co-Founder - CANIT SOLUTIONS, CEO – THINKCOMM MARKETING & MEDIA SERVICES PVT LTD., is an author of 2 successful book **"Grad to Professional"** & **"Secret of Professional Intrapreneur"**, of which is the first purely for college grads to get ready for the professional world outside, and the second is completely for working professionals and secrets to succussed, this book **"MMM"** along with his Co-Author **Sachin Sajan** is of a complete different genre which gives the readers a flavour of the given topics from a very different perspective, he also has lots more planned to be released. He comes with more than a decade of experience with Eye for winning process flow. Engaged in different brand journcys over 15years in marketing and analysing customer psychology.

CHAPTER SIXTEEN

ABOUT THE CO-AUTHOR – Sachin Sajan

Sachin is a published author of two anthology books for which he had written and shared his short stories and poetries. A man with many hats for each occasion as his belief is, that there's one life then why shy away from doing things which excite him. Working on **"MMM"** was one such exciting venture.

Printed by Libri Plureos GmbH in Hamburg,
Germany